TIMES OF FLOOD

A PORTRAIT OF THE FENLAND DROWNS
IN OLD PRINTS AND PHOTOGRAPHS

Anthony Day

S.B. Publications

By the same author:
Wicken: A Fen Village (1990)
Fen and Marshland Villages (1993)
But For Such Men As These (1994)
Farming in the Fens (1995)
Wicken: A Second Portrait of a Fen Village (1996)

In tribute to Walter Martin Lane, who was there for us all

First published in 1997 by S.B. Publications
℅ 19 Grove Road, Seaford, East Sussex BN25 1TP.

ISBN: 1 85770 119 4

Typeset, printed and bound by
Manchester Free Press,
Longford Trading Estate,
Thomas Street, Stretford,
Manchester M32 0JT.
Tel: 0161 864 4540.

CONTENTS

Front Cover: One Haddenham farmer, Tom Burton,
looks resignedly upon the wrecked house of another, Arthur Thulbon,
during the floods of 1947, the worst on record in the fens.
A gale preceded the floods and strong winds continued to batter the
properties along Hillrow and Hillrow Causeway and those below
Sutton so that the farmers, deprived of a cropping year,
had to be rescued by a relief fund.

Cambridgeshire Collection: W. Martin Lane

INTRODUCTION

Those worthy 19th century historians, S.H. Miller and S.B.J. Skertchly, described the fens of long ago as a vast open plain covered with deep sedge, with thickets of alder and willow, abounding in shallow lakes temporary and permanent, where the drier parts provided luxurious pastures in summer and where the water level rose and spread in winter

Thinly populated, its inhabitants of mixed descent had long adapted to living on the secure silt levels while depending on the resources below. They fed on fish and wildfowl, took the reeds and sedge for their shelters and ultimately discovered their source of fuel in dried peat. They were contemptuous of 'uplanders' and wary of any incursion into their amphibious way of life.

Their region had been created by an ice age in thaw that left Britain an island. A huge inrush of sea crushed all before it and brought the level of the land down to become a fen. To the settlers there the sea was friend, safeguarding their livelihood, but to others it was and remains the enemy. The Romans built barriers against it to reclaim marshland but the sea broke past them all too often and subsequent attempts to drain the fens in part were limited enough to offer no threat to the settlers.

The Duke of Bedford changed all that in the reign of Charles I. He and his Company of Adventurers entrusted their ambitious drainage scheme to the Dutch engineer, Sir Cornelius Vermuyden, who had already taken English nationality and had received a knighthood for his success in draining Hatfield Chase in Yorkshire which he began in 1626. Once their scheme became reality the fenmen rebelled. They attacked the new dykes and embankments as they were being created and were warlike in their resort to pikes and stones against the figures of authority. But these amphibians were destined to transform gradually into farmers, although they clung to old ways in using the new channels, the rivers and washes for their fish and wildfowl.

The fens extend for seventy miles between Cambridge and Lincoln and are thirty-five miles wide reaching into Marshland, reclaimed directly from the sea. Four main rivers govern the drainage, in part natural but greatly altered by man. The most northern is the Witham from Lincoln to Boston.

Southwards there is the Welland, rising in Northamptonshire and passing Stamford to Spalding and on to The Wash. Then comes The Nene through Peterborough to Wisbech and on through an artificial channel to The Wash, while the most southerly and the biggest is The Great Ouse, rising also in Northamptonshire, travelling through Buckinghamshire, Bedfordshire and Huntingdonshire to Earith where it divides into three channels.

Vermuyden's scheme began here in Earith before the civil war. The Old Bedford River was cut from here to Denver in Norfolk twenty-two miles away and after the civil war, under the Commonwealth and using prisoners of war, the New Bedford River or Hundredfoot Drain was cut parallel with a wide stretch of washland in between to take the surplus water in season. The Old Bedford, which is now of little significance to the drainage scheme, is controlled by a sluice at Earith and the Hundredfoot is tidal, bypassing the great sluice at Denver. The Ouse course continues as The Old West River until it joins The Cam beyond Stretham when it become The Ely Ouse. It takes in the tributaries of The River Lark at Prickwillow, The Little Ouse at Brandon Creek and The Wissey at Hilgay and hereabouts it is known as The Ten Mile River until it becomes The Great Ouse passing Denver, St. Germans which controls the Middle Level and King's Lynn into The Wash.

Vermuyden's scheme, dividing the fens into the South, Middle and North Levels, was meant to provide only summer land. Bringing the land into cultivation in winter was never in his mind, although the fens at that time were above mean tide level. His improved channelling took the water away by natural fall, but little was understood about the effects of water velocity or the accumulation of silt under those conditions. The outfalls, indeed, soon became clogged and the scheme faltered. Vermuyden's scheme, which was never entirely his own, was regarded unfavourably for a long time but later opinion has favoured him and his plans for further channels have since been carried out.

The enterprise was disastrous for Veymuyden himself, leaving him in poverty and his backers in ruin, the land apportioned to them as recompense serving them ill. A subsequent disadvantage to the scheme, unconsidered by Vermuyden, was the erosion of the dry peat after drainage, causing the level to sink until it was below the river levels. Horse-powered pumps had to be installed to lift the water, then a legion of windmills that continued to serve a subsidiary role after the advent of the steam age.

More and more drains were cut to keep the fens dry and the crisis for steam came when the scoopwheels could be lowered no further to counter the shrinkage of the surface. Diesel pumps were installed in time to avert crisis, then electric power took over to great effect. No flood crisis has occurred in the fens since electricity took over, despite national power crises, but the sea in the meantime has confined its ravages to the coastal communities, most catastrophically on February 1st 1953. Flood crises occur when the high tides block the outlets to The Wash and the rivers fill to overflowing or burst their banks. Heavy rain or strong winds generally accompany such conditions and the outcome is another drown, the word chosen by fenmen as more appropriate than inundation or flood.

In Marshland the sea has reclaimed its own many times since the Roman occupation, sometimes sending its inhabitants fleeing to the church towers for safety. In 1713 a torrent of tidal water smashed Denver Sluice and the fens reverted for thirty-five years before a new sluice was built. The Hundredfoot, so vital to the South Level, burst its banks in 1799, 1805 and 1809, swamping above six thousand acres each time and there have been many breaches in other river banks since. Heavy rainfall augurs enough trouble for the fen farmers but burst banks spell ruin. The last fenland drown and the worst on record occurred in 1947. This book commemorates its fiftieth anniversary.

CHARM OF THE FENS

Covering some 1,300 square miles, the fens form England's broadest plain, most of it under intense cultivation. Drainage transformed it into a man-made landscape sectioned by straight dykes and drains between the winding rivers and ever rising embankments to counter the shrinkage of the peat. For it is a disappearing landscape, destined to erode down to the clay. People tend to love or loathe the region, but it still has its charms and artists over the years have discovered them - even idealised them like Robert MacBeth R.A. who found them through his friend and fellow artist, Robert Farren of Cambridge. This is a composite scene from the 1880s showing what nature and man had done together to give it appeal.

Author's Collection: Robert MacBeth R.A.

THE FENS FOR LEISURE

Men from the Cambridgeshire villages of Wicken, Soham, Swaffham Prior, Swaffham Bulbeck and Bottisham were at the heart of the rebellion against fen drainage in the 17th century, but where other villages lost so much of what they held dear the men of Wicken were left with a sense of triumph. An expanse of primeval fen was left undrained to ensure that life in the village should change but slowly. Although the character of the fen has been changed by the surrounding drainage it remains today as an attraction for thousands of visitors each year.

When in 1919 the Reverend Edwin Lewis became vicar of Wicken his enthusiasm for his new surroundings persuaded him to invite his old congregation over from Luton to enjoy the different landscape and its attractions. Here they are aboard two barges, manned by Bill Barnes the Wicken Fen keeper, holding the barge pole, with the vicar near him in a straw hat. This is Wicken Lode that meanders its way past the fen into Burwell Lode which continues to Upware and the Cam where no doubt this human cargo enjoyed the delights of the then famous inn, the 'Five Miles from Anywhere - No Hurry.' The lodes hereabouts are no longer part of the drainage system but are preserved for the fishing and boating enthusiasts. When the rivers of the fens were used constantly for transportation the many riverside inns were busier than any inland.

Author's Collection

SUNDAY SILENCE

The fertile peat grew weeds as successfully as corn or root crops and fen farmers had to work very hard for success throughout the kindest of seasons. The fens, however, offer a peaceful aspect even today while before the machine age they were silence itself. This view at Barway, a hamlet near Ely, catches the tranquillity of late afternoon on a summer Sunday in the 1930s. The cows are being milked on a day when work is limited to the tending of livestock, where the visitor feels entitled to wear his leisure suit at the scene of work. Not far from this spot the floods of 1937 did great damage to the prospects of this farmer and his like.

Cambridgeshire Collection

WORK FOR THEM ALL

Living in the fens meant working in the fens. Commuting to jobs in the towns had to wait for the omnibus age and girls who wanted other than land work before marriage went into service in the big houses. When harvesting was done by hand there was work for all, including the housewives who enjoyed the part-time seasonal jobs such as potato, carrot and strawberry picking for the extra pay and the comradeship. They were used to bending and crawling to do these jobs and I know people today who miss the company of the land and reflect little on the rigours of the work. This is a proudly displayed sample of a fine crop of potatoes early this century, to which the photographer had been called by the farmer. While the floods stay away such crops are standard today when, conversely, irrigation is much used to bring them along. Groups of workers can still be seen in the lettuce fields but machines do most of the jobs.

Cambridgeshire Collection

FUEL FROM THE FENS

It was a dense forest region before that tremendous interglacial tide swept the trees down and created the fens. Those trees have been rising to the surface ever since, known as bog oaks, but where living trees were scarce the fenmen had to search for something else for fuel. They found it, a long time ago, in the underlying peat, a commodity generally referred to by fenmen as turf. It was dug all over the fens, dried thoroughly and placed on the open hearths in stacks to smoulder for days on end. In the small shelters and cottages the freezing winters became warm and turf digging became a thriving industry serving the towns.

This turf digger is in Adventurers' Fen near Burwell in the 1920s when there was still considerable demand for turf although the industry had been in decline since the turn of the century. He would be working for piecework wages digging, stacking, opening the turfs to dry sooner and transporting to large stacks or by boat to the turf sheds. They dug deep for the turf in this fen, leaving it a bog ideal for wildlife afterwards until it was reclaimed for agriculture during the second world war.

Cambridgeshire Collection

TURF BOGS

Showing clearly enough here is the pride in workmanship typical of the full-time turf digger. These bogs are at Lapwing in Burwell Fen, owned by the Wicken builder and carpenter. Josiah Owers, who was a native of Birmingham. The turf digging season hereabouts lasted from the first week in March to the last week in August and the digging was done with a becket, a slim spade like a cricket bat with a right-angled flange to ensure two cuts to the thrust, The peat from the depth it was dug was soft and the thrust came only from the arms. The turves generally dried within six weeks and were sold by the hundred. When Wicken's turf diggers took to using a larger becket they sold only sixty turves to the hundred, yet they were still referred to as hundreds. Flooding here outside the digging season was encouraged to keep out the moles and worms. Owers built his own drainage mill, seen in the distance by Commissioners' Drain running alongside Burwell Lode. The March winds soon enabled it to dry out the bogs, as they were called.

Birmingham Library Service: P.J. Deakin.

HOME IN THE FENS

The finest farmhouses in the fen region are invariably built on the high secure ground Those on fen level are ever at risk not only from flooding but subsidence. 'Leaners' were once a feature of the fens while other houses cracked down the middle. Buttressing generally did more to pull the leaner down than prop it up and there were remarkable examples of patching-up long after the house was unfit for human habitation. They were never old houses. Wooden houses had greater longevity, often topped with corrugated iron for extra discomfort from the cold in winter and the heat in summer. Tar was applied against the winds and driving rain. They were often derided as 'castles' or 'halls'!

Here is a typically dishevelled fen farmstead near Ely, privacy guaranteed in winter by the approach road. The house, looking the worse for wear, was an ambitious one for the site and the evidence of livestock is not supported by the accommodation. Such smallholdings were often placed by the waterways, the only source of water at this time, c.1930, for man or beast. Too much of that in the river put it well above the level of the yard and the ground floor. Today homes on fen level are built on concrete rafts and they are very often bungalows.

Cambridgeshire Collection

THE WASHLAND

The fen rivers are served by washes with floodbanks to contain the excess water in season. The washland between the Bedford Rivers extends to 4,600 acres which, however wet the winters, becomes in summer the luxurious pastureland of pre-drainage fenland. Some parts left for hay become cattle pastures with the rest afterwards, although at Welney the washes have been acquired as a sanctuary for waterbirds and there is a viewing platform for those wanting to see the winter visitors being fed. The washes, 22 miles long, are more than half a mile wide in places. The Old and New Bedford Rivers join at Welmore Sluice a little more than a mile from Denver. The cattle mourn across these washes today just as they at the time of this view c.1930.

Cambridgeshire Collection: D.G. Reid

DRAINAGE: WINDPOWER

The windmills that drained the fens for close on 250 years were finely constructed and made to last. Such millwrights are a lost breed, so that when the National Trust decided to restore the last drainage windmill left standing near Wicken Fen they had to call in a carpenter, nearing the end of his working life, to do the job. He, C.J. Ison of Histon, did a magnificent job and the windmill stands in the fen as much a memorial to him as to Lord Fairhaven who financed the enterprise.

This beautiful example, Harrimere Mill, on Soham Lode by the Ely Ouse served for a long time to drain Soham Mere. It was demolished in 1917 and its successor today is a characterless house of brick. The overseer of Harrimere lived in a bungalow nearby. His mill, he knew, was made strong and he knew too when maintenance was due. When the mill was needed cloths, or sweeps, were attached to the sails, the brake was released and away it went - sometimes too fast when the wind was strong. The cap was adjusted to the wind by hand. Great stress was put on the scoopwheel slapping the water upwards for hours on end, but they were made to withstand it. A sluice controlled the level of the lode here.

Cambridgeshire Collection

STEAMPOWER

From the 1820s steampower took over the draining of the fens. The tall-chimneyed, coal-fired pumping stations proliferated beside the rivers, although the windmills remained to lift the water from the smaller drains. This is the Swaffham Engine at Upware in the 1920s, at the head of the Swaffham Fen Drain where it pumped the water up to the Cam level. This engine was installed in 1850, replacing another in a different shed built in 1821. It was demolished in 1939. An electrical installation stands on the site today with the replacement diesel shed, built in 1927, still standing. Another pumping station, the Burwell Engine, operated close by at the head of Commissioners' Drain and the building still stands. Not far away, by the Old West River, stands Stretham Old Engine, built in 1831 and left as an example of its kind and open to visitors. It last operated during the Second World War.

Cambridgeshire Collection

WILLIAM STEVENS

These fens oft-times have been by water drowned,
Science a remedy in water found,
The power of steam, she said, shall be employed
And the destroyer by itself destroyed.

Thus the tenor of a poetic Commissioner of Drainage, inscribed on the wall of the Hundredfoot pumping station near Little Downham where served William Stevens as engineer until he took over the Swaffham Engine at Upware between 1881 and 1906. Trained as a blacksmith, he became also the District Superintendent and was succeeded by his son, Arthur, as engineer. Such men carried huge responsibilities, particularly in times of flood crisis and William was to have his mettle tested by a near catastrophe in 1897. Men of his ilk knew every sound and breath their great engines should make and were ever on the alert for problems. William was a proud man, guarding his knowledge even from his own son and assistant; but the young man learned enough to take over.

Author's Collection

THE ENGINE

The massive beam engines that secured the drainage of the fens for more than a century were superbly wrought. Their reliability was essential and although mechanical problems did occur the engineers were generally well on top of them. This is a glance at the Swaffham Engine at Upware in 1896, the details of it assembled by Keith Hinde of Waterbeach:

A single cylinder condensing beam engine driving a scoopwheel, it was made by Robert Daglish and Company of St. Helens. Bore: 42 inches. Strokes 84 inches. Diameter of flywheel 25 feet. Diameter of crankshafts 14 inches. Beams 22^1/$_2$ feet, Speeds approximately 15 r.p.m. Boilers: two Galloway. Pressure: up to 35/40 pounds per square inch. Scoopwheel diameter: 36 feet. Paddles: 48, each 5 feet-9 inches long by 3 feet-6 inches wide. Date last worked: 1937. Date of demolitions 1939. The engine drivers were: Charles Chapman (also District Superintendent) 1877-1881; William Stevens (also District Superintendent) 1881-1906; Arthur Stevens 1906-1932; Charles Bullman 1932-1937.

Cambridgeshire Collection

THE BEAM

Inspired as much as dictated by functional need, our great engineers must have felt artistic satisfaction in creating such forms as this beam at the Swaffham Engine, photographed in the 1920s. It was a massive experience to see it working and it is small wonder those fen pumping stations were built like lay chapels, reverently designed. The hymns, however, resonating like great sighs, were in tribute to steam, a form of propulsion that today is beheld with great reference by a legion of nostalgic enthusiasts responding to the true sound of power. No boy could respond to a diesel-electric train as we once did to the steam locomotive, waiting to carry us into the blue.

Rosa Stevens

THE BALANCE WHEEL

Maintenance, well in advance of any urgent need, was the key to longevity in engines. Boilers had to be replaced, scoopwheels repaired, enlarged or replaced and engines repaired and modified. Yet, to the shame of the engineer, breakdowns occurred such as that at the Swaffham Engine on February 10th 1897. This in spite of it being one of the last of its type to be installed in the fens - and one of the best. In the year after it was built Appold's centrifugal pump was displayed at the Great Exhibition and was immediately installed at Whittlesey Mere. The Swaffham Engine cost £9,000.

Forced to keep in going to defeat the waters of 1897, William Stevens heard the crankshaft snap under the strain, leaving the huge cast-iron connecting rod to swing wildly around, crashing against the wall. To shut the steam off quickly William had to get past the crippled machinery into the boiler house before returning to slow the engine down. 64 at the time, he managed the job without injury with the help of the stoker who had to rake out the hot coals until he was about to roast to death. William made an inspired guess as to when to shut down the engine and was a hero for his efforts. Since it took five weeks to get a portable engine installed the region went under water for that time. Originally powered by steam, the adjacent Burwell engine changed to gas, became prone to fires and suffered a bad one in 1913 after which, for a time, it ran on paraffin. This photograph of the Swaffham Engine balance wheel was taken in 1927, the year that diesel was installed.

Rosa Stevens

THE STOKERS

Working in such warm conditions, the stokers in the pumping stations were apt to feel the elements outside. It was warm enough in the Swaffham Engine house for Arthur Stevens, a passionate gardener, to grow an orange tree successfully. In this picture, however, the scene is the Hundredfoot Engine serving the Littleport and Downham District early this century, with the stokers standing nicely still for a clear picture.

The first steam pump in the fens was installed at Sutton St. Edumds in 1817 and the oldest example existing to day is the Stretham Old Engine. Once the technology had been introduced into the fens more than fifty pumping stations were built in the southern fens alone, replacing in their lifting power some two thousand windmills.

Cambridgeshire Collection

THE SCOOPWHEEL

This is the scoopwheel under construction, the instrument on which the fens depended for so long for successful drainage. What sculptural satisfaction must have gone into creating such a masterpiece! What standards of craftsmanship every plain man and every apprentice had to live up to in those times! Could any man make such a construction any more? This scoopwheel was being made, on August 31st 1900, for the Third District Commissioners at Whittlesey and it was designed and built by Herbert J. Varlow, engineer, of March. Better not reflect on what such a job would cost today - if it could be done!

Cambridgeshire Collection

INTO DIESEL

The transfer from steam to diesel power proceeded apace in the 1920s and it was something to celebrate in the fens. The change came at a crucial time, when the scoopwheels of the steam pumps could be lowered no further without widespread rebuilding. At Prickwillow near Ely where two engine houses were built side by side, the first in 1831 and the second in 1880, the second one had a centrifugal pump, but in 1924 a five-cylinder Mirrless diesel engine was installed, at a time when diesel oil was much cheaper than coal. The scene here is the formal opening of the outlet for the engine into the River Lark in 1926. Increased performance was always of intense interest to fen people looking for greater security from floods.

Cambridgeshire Collection

THE PUDDLERS

These men are engaged in puddling the banks of Bottisham Lode in 1898, although in needing to raise the bank higher they are using more clay than would normally be required to make the bank waterproof. Dredgers could lift enough clay from the lode for most puddling jobs, but that here came from a pit dug for the purpose. A hard job indeed, like most jobs of waterway maintenance in the fens. In the boats are, left to right; Bill Barnes, who then lived at 'The Anchor' public house in Upware and who later became the first keeper of Wicken Fen; Jack Howe of 'The Cherry Tree' public house in Swaffham Pen; Buck Whitehead, and Arthur Stevens who assisted his father at the Swaffham Engine but was a general employee of the drainage board. Fourth from the left at the back is Arthur's brother, Charlie. They belonged, to a closely-knit community at Upware, their second home in most cases being the 'Five Miles from Anywhere - No Hurry.'

Author's Collection

THE SLUBBERS

Drainage channels have to be kept clear and deep to serve the system and while this is done mechanically now so much had to be done by hand as here in the 1890s, one of the most painfully laborious jobs imaginable. The word slub is an alternative for mud or ooze and, the principal tool for this was the scoop, Slubbing has to be done even in the channels within Wicken Fen to prevent the reeds taking over. When dredgers came in they put a lot of men out of work, but it is hard to imagine a man complaining about having to give up a job like this.

Cambridgeshire Collection

DREDGING

This is a floating steam dragline, numbered OBD No 6, at work on the Ouse near Clayway between Queen Adelaide and Littleport in the 1930s. I quote from a very young 90-years old Albert Gee from Thorney in 1996:

'I was a farm boy in 1919 and learnt to drive a 1917 Fordson tractor in my school holidays, but when I left school at 13, I had to work among the horses, learn to plough, etcetera. Later I was put on a tractor full time but I got restive for a change. I decided that farm work was very hard. I then got a job as a labourer on the dredging and widening scheme to allow sea-going craft up from Wisbech and Peterborough docks. I soon found this harder work than on any farm. Most of the men were Dutch labourers and they were a very hard lot. I later joined a drainage contracting firm as a dragline driver and worked on several schemes in the southern fens. I then went to all parts of the country, working on aerodromes and army camps. I came home to the depot when the 1947 floods occurred but was made a maintenance fitter to maintain the draglines working on the floods. We opened two clay pits to repair the banks, one at Peakirk and the other at Crowland where the ground gave way and pitched a dragline upside down in the pit. The driver jumped for his life and was unhurt but I had a very battered machine to put to work again.'

Cambridgeshire Collection

THE OSIER MATS

Damming remains a part of waterway maintenance and use is still made of the osier mat, a means introduced by the Dutchmen who still play a part in our fen drainage. Osiers are plaited into rafts which are sunk with heavy stones, such as are being thrown on to this one from the barge. The mats are used one on top of the other for dams or for healing a breach in a river bank. Heaps of clay were also deposited near the river banks in case of an emergency breach, but when such occurred it was in flood crisis and there was never enough clay handy to do the job. More had to be fetched in worsening conditions, if possible by barge, but at a tedious pace. Forward planning was never enough in times of flood.

Cambridgeshire Collection

THE NAVVIES

They liked to be called workmen, but their superiors dubbed them navvies and one of the gang shown here, L. Hall of Swavesey, explains the job in hand: 'On the Old West River from Earith to Aldreth bridge and onward we had to dig by hand-forks and spades a trench four feet deep and two feet wide, river side of the bank. A crane unloaded the gault (clay) from the barges, dropped it into the trench and then we had to level it and tread it down with our boots. The crane travelled along near the river edge on thick wooden mats, about four inches thick. The mats were about four feet by eight feet As the crane moved forward the mats had to be moved from the rear and placed in front of the crane. The trench was filled with gault and sloped up the bank to raise it by two feet After this the bank had to be covered with topsoil. We worked from 7a.m. to 4p.m. with half an hour for dockey, all for three pounds a week, which was very good pay then, as farmworkers' pay was then thirty shillings.' Mr. Hall explained the job thus in 1986 when he was 75.

Cambridgeshire Collection

DENVER SLUICE

The great sluice at Denver may never have been in Vermuyden's plans for draining the South Level. It was projected by a Colonel William Dodson and was to serve the purpose of preventing the tidal silt from entering the Great Ouse and to preclude the need to raise and reinforce its banks to contain the tidal levels. It was first constructed in 1651 and was reconstructed in 1682 to the design of Sir Thomas Fitch. Completely destroyed in 1713, it was not rebuilt until 1751, to the design of Charles Labelye who designed the first Westminster Bridge over the Thames. Bitter controversy had turned to general agreement that it was necessary in face of the condition of the level between-times and the presence of the new Hundredfoot Drain cut by Vermuyden. The drainage of the level has certainly generated more problems than the Middle and North Levels but it depends largely on this sluice today, courtesy of the mood of the sea. This view of the sluice comes from the 1880s when the rivers were busy, but it looks very different today with its updated apparatus.

Central Divisional Library, King's Lynn; Taylor Slide Collection

GUARDIANS OF THE SLUICE

This is Denver Sluice in 1902, showing the muscle-power needed by the operator. He is overseen here by George Carmichael, consulting engineer to the Burnt Fen Commissioners, a man with big responsibilities. Vermuyden's scheme, whether it envisaged a sluice here or not, has engendered controversy ever since. Although he split the fens into three levels he saw, from the lessons of previous attempts to drain the fens in part, that they had to be interdependent.

The two Bedford rivers were not his original idea but he made use of them and wished to continue with a cut-off channel relieving the Rivers Lark, Little Ouse and Wissey and taken beyond Denver, plus a relief channel for the Ouse beyond there and schemes approximating to these were carried out in the 1960s. This might imply advocacy for Vermuyden's scheme or simply extending what was in place ~but his was the mastermind upon which we still depend. Long after he had departed the fens returned to a parlous state due to the shrinkage of the peat, but if Vermuyden had not envisaged this he knew that advancing science would reinforce his scheme.

Cambridgeshire Collection

ST. GERMAN'S SLUICE

The South Level Commissioners have had reason to envy those of the North and Middle Levels for their relative freedom from drainage problems over the years. Control of the Middle Level waters is asserted here at St. German's near King's Lynn and four miles along from Denver. Here it takes the water from the Middle Level Drain into the Great Ouse and it has a history of increasing success. There was a disaster here in 1862 when the sluice of the Marshland Cut collapsed under the pressure of the inrushing tide but the situation has been under control since. The main sluice collapsed in the 1880s but was reparable, the sealed cracks remaining visible on the walls for years after. This present structure was built in 1934, capable of lifting 3,000 tons of water a minute.

Cambridgeshire Collection

THE MARSHLAND SLUICE

Wet or snowbound winters put fenmen on their guard for subsequent floods but they felt entitled to freedom from fear throughout the summer. Yet the vagaries of the weather and certainly the tides could never ensure them comfort even then. While the crops were advancing nicely, on the fen soil there came a dramatic intervention on May 4th 1862 when the incoming tide roared down the Marshland Cut and crashed through the sluice at the Middle Level Drain, filled the drain and burst through its banks to flood 8,000 acres. It spelt ruin for many and acute discomfort long after the waters receded. The artist of the London Illustrated News went along to draw this impression of the broken sluice.

Cambridgeshire Collection

THE MIDDLE LEVEL FLOODED

There is not much drama to be captured in a sparsely populated area of the fens in flood. The artist here might have been drawing for the leisure industry; there is almost a 'come and be enchanted' feel about the view. He draws meticulously and precisely, showing the breach in the Middle Level bank in 1862 that spread the waters across the farmland, but drama there is none, such as accompanied the burst and no sense of the sorrow felt by the victims.

Cambridgeshire Collection

THE DESERTED FARMSTEAD

Within hours the prospects for a successful farming year had gone, without hope of compensation. Again the artist turns it into a charming scene at odds with the reality of the moment. The accompanying journalist had a different story to tell in words. He underlined the doom and gloom. He watched the wind stir the water in this year of 1862 'making the waves look as if they had been accustomed to rollick and grow vengeful there for ages.' He did his best to feel some of the despair of the fenmen, caught by the spring tides in the season of blossom. The calamity was not quite as dire as he and others reported, but it was bad enough.

Cambridgeshire Collection

RECONSTRUCTION

The Middle Level Drain was completed in 1848, providing the level with a point of discharge into the Great Ouse estuary about six miles farther downstream than before which provided an additional fall of some six feet. The improvement in drainage that followed from 1851 engendered plans to drain Whittlesey Mere, but the inhabitants of Marshland opposed the Middle Level Act embodying this, believing the waters would be diverted their way to cause havoc. The drainage went ahead without mishap although a wonderful habitat was destroyed. The mere spread over 1,600 acres although in summer this shrank to some 1,000 acres, a place where boating and skating abounded in season. The farmers' troubles in May 1862 had, however, stemmed straight from the sea and it was imperative the coffer-dam should be rebuilt to withstand all its pressures. Work on this began quickly and the activity of building it is caught here by a fine draughtsman.

Cambridgeshire Collection

THE NORTH LEVEL DROWN OF 1880

The North Level lies between the Welland and the Nene, the Middle Level between the Nene and the Old Bedford River and the South Level extends from there to the high land. Crowland in south Lincolnshire is the scene depicted here, in October 1880, a time of heavy constant rain that put the banks of the Welland and Nene under great strain. There was overflowing and vast spreads of water occurred in the North Level. The floods touched Spalding, Bourne and Peterborough and went as far as Huntingdon, St. Ives and Godmanchester. Breaches occurred near Spalding and Bourne, repairs to which put such a strain on the sluice on the River Glen that it gave way. On the night of Saturday 9th October the bank of the Welland gave way near Becken's Mill. Hordes of workmen fought to repair the breach using sacks of earth but they could only watch the water pouring over the banks. A Wisbech firm, Dawbarn and Sons, donated 9,000 sacks for the purpose. North-east winds worsened the damage and bank gave way further to create the worst floods in the area since 1796. There was corn still uncut and root crops perishing and there were outcries for the drainage system to be improved. Once more the artist's sympathy for the plight of the inhabitants hardly shows in a scene drawn for its beauty. The first North Level sluice was built in 1830.

Cambridgeshire Collection

PEAKIRK

The drown of 1880 here reaches the village of Peakirk near Peterborough and the artist draws it as a scene enhanced by the floods. Once more the reporters gave the facts with sympathy for the sufferers, but the moment needed a photographer to get nearer the anguish of the inhabitants. Happily the northeast winds that had forced the water along the Welland soon eased. Crowland had some 3,000 inhabitants at this time. There are ruins there of the abbey founded by Ethelbald, king of Mercia, in honour of Saint Guthlac, who had lived there long before. Saint Guthlac's sister, Pega, lived six miles away at Pega's Kirk, named after the chapel she founded there. Thus is became Peakirk with a population in 1880 of around 250. It remains a small village, less vulnerable to flooding today when its population is around 330.

Cambridgeshire Collection

A DRY HARVEST

In the generally dry conditions that usually prevail in August and September the harvesting scene in the fens appeared like this, the hard work progressing in an atmosphere of tranquillity. Small fields sheltered by high hedges prevailed until the heavy machinery was introduced, to serve which the fields were laid bare - and barer still when the Spring and Autumn winds came to lift the dry peat into dust-storms. The harvests before that went on for a good six weeks with the men working twelve hours a day, Sundays always excluded. There were bad seasons when the rain had flattened the corn and men had to go back to scythes but the floods of 1880 and the deluge of 1912 were totally unexpected setbacks.

Cambridgeshire Collection: C.G.M. Hatfield

A FLOODED COIN FIELD. AUGUST 1912.

A WET HARVEST

So to the most unexpected fenland drown. There were countrywide storms, making fenmen fear the worst and the farmer owning this field had to bring his corn away in a boat. On Monday August 26th 1912 came the tropical deluge that lasted twelve hours, producing six inches of rain before four p.m., leaving the were region a vast lake. Corn shooks swam, late hay fields were ruined and many root crops had to be left to rot. Afterwards blight affected the potatoes and several small farmers were ruined. The field shown here is in Ramsey, Huntingdonshire and there were many more like it.

Cambridgeshire Collection

The River Ouse Bank Bursted near Lakenheath 1912

THE BREACH IN THE LITTLE OUSE

There are high tides in August but seldom such downpours as those of 1912 to put the drainage system to the test at that time. The rivers swelled, the banks burst and the force of the water is evident in this scene near Lakenheath where the Little Ouse breaks through. Crops were abandoned, the climax of the farming year written off in many places. Any corn that was not swept away had sprouted green by the time the floods cleared. The stormy conditions continued through most of September. Torrents shooting down the Yare at Norwich carried driftwood enough to smash the bridges, but one man there, Harry Abel, a corporation official, risked his life to attach ropes to floating timbers so that they could be pulled back from the bridge they were threatening It was estimated there were 350 tons of water per acre around Chatteris and all the cattle had to be moved from the Bedford washes, some to Ely, and it was several weeks before the floods subsided.

Cambridgeshire Collection

THE OUSE BANK GIVES WAY

It was a unique experience for these men to be attending a breach in a river bank in August. The storms of August 1912 forced the Ouse bank near Hilgay, Norfolk, to give way, adding to the floods that had already formed after those storms. Official figures showed that the river level rose to sixteen feet, six-and-a-half inches above the normal where the previous highest was fifteen feet-six-and-a-half inches in the year 1614 It was estimated that £27,860 would be needed to effect drainage repairs in Norfolk.

Cambridgeshire Collection

FLOODS AT ELY

To those who know it and to those who see it for the first time Ely Cathedral is one of the wonders of the land. Begun three years before the great undertaking of the Domesday Book, it was nearly a century later when the roof timbers were in position a hundred feet above the floor and it has features unsurpassed for beauty. Ely like its surrounding islands of Wibburton and Haddenham, Coveney, Little Downham and Littleport, stands safely above the incursion of floods but they have often occurred around its feet. This scene at Annesdale by the Cam has occurred many times over the years, attracting photographers in recent times for the sheer beauty of the scene. The Cam has gone over the quay to the Cutter Inn early this century, a seasonal hazard.

Cambridgeshire Collection

HIGH WATER IN 1928

The South Level banks came under pressure again in January 1928, one of the three months of grave expectation in the fens. The scene here is the Little Ouse at Botany Bay near Lakenheath on January 7th, the river bank broken and the waters escaping while the steam pump and the windmill side by side stand helpless while the tidal pressures prevent the outflow. The breach was soon mended but the threat of further bank erosion remained for some weeks and the land was waterlogged for weeks.

Cambridgeshire Collection

The 12.15 from Littleport going through the floods. Jan. 1928

WINTER TRAVEL

I doubt if many Littleport people took advantage of the railway service between King's Lynn and London in the middle of winter in 1928. Those were not commuting days as we know them, but the service to Ely and Cambridge, where some local people worked, was already essential. In January 1928 they rode over the waters for a long way and came home hoping to see them receding. The River Cam was in torrent, described at the time as an eight-miles-an-hour 'hustle' in Cambridge. The north bank of the River Wissey $1^1/2$ miles below Hillgay burst its banks and flooded a thousand acres. The river was fifty-one feet wide at that point and twenty-three feet deep to the very top of the bank. There had been a gale Friday January 6th to give the menace a boost.

Cambridgeshire Collection

THE RIVER TRAFFIC THWARTED

Rises in the river levels in winter disrupted the barge and maintenance traffic and there was plenty of it still in January 1928. Tugs and barges were needed to repair the river banks, but they could come to grief like this one at the Brandon Creek bridge, which could only wait until the river went down. Leisure traffic on the rivers was on the increase at this time but there was little of it in winter. Problems accrued when the sea tried to reclaim its own.

Cambridgeshire Collection

WELNEY

Floods are an acceptable phenomenon in the fens - when they occur in the places set aside for them. The river washes are there to take the overflow, none more obviously than the Bedford or Ouse washes, but the highways across them are meant to stay high and dry. The floods, however, have often risen above the crossings at Earith, Sutton Gault, Mepal and Welney which is shown here during the troublesome winter of 1928. Time then to take to the road in boats which were always on standby and part of a way of life. These boys may not have seen it like this before, but they would certainly see it again. Water there is good news for those in charge of today's Welney Wildlife Reserve and the hundreds of visitors who arrive to watch the waterfowl feeding.

Lillian Ream

GETTING IN SUPPLIES

Once more the flood level is higher than normal in the Bedford washes, cutting off the outside world for pedestrians and cyclists. Cars there were few at this time in the 1920s but steam had been around a long time and could be turned to various uses, including the fetching of supplies through the water. The fifth route across the washes is the Cambridge-Peterborough railway near Black Bank and the Downham engine which remains high and dry. At Sutton Gault a wooden walkway was built above the usual flood level. The traction engine had power enough to pull two laden wagons and more and it was on standby for such times as this, when not driving a threshing drum.

Cambridgeshire Collection

TRANQUIL WATERS

This is nearer the normal level between the Bedford rivers whose inner banks are left low to allow the overflow into the washes and there is seldom a winter when they are not covered. This scene from the 1920s at Mepal offers no threat. It is just a normal, tranquil scene for the photographer, catching the horse and cart going at a leisurely place. These are friendly waters, although fen children were made to realise that water was both friend and enemy, good for fishing, bathing and skating, bad for its capacity to chill, infect and drown. There were flood crises enough to keep them aware, drownings enough to scare them.

Cambridgeshire Collection

COWBIT WASH

The long stretch of Cowbit Wash by the River Welland between Crowland and Spalding is another reservoir for overflow, where men are prepared for it with boats. Sheds such as that shown are the only habitations, apart from singular example of a gypsy caravan left over from summer. This is 1932, the rainfall about average, the flood no more than normal, the sequel a rich crops of grass for the cattle.

Lilian Ream

THE FLOOD PUMPS

In the winter of 1937 there were impassioned pleas in the House of Commons from members of parliament on behalf of the fen farmers around Ely who were in another flood crisis. The sea was blocking the way out again, the waters of the Cam lapping the tops of the banks. There had been five previous flood crises in the area this century but the water levels had never been higher - three-and-a-half inches above the previous record. The Cam, however, held firm while overflowing and the government did offer assistance. A war was on its way and natural disasters on this regional scale would soon slip out of the headlines. The scene here is Upware, with an auxiliary pump putting the Cam under more strain.

Cambridgeshire Collection: C.G.M. Hatfield

NOT BEER, BUT OIL

Almost 8,000 acres of agricultural land was flooded at Cottenham, near Cambridge, in March 1937. However, there had been complaints about the drainage of this area for a long time. It was flooded damagingly in 1911, 1919 and 1928 and there were loud claims that the Upware pumps were not powerful enough to keep the land dry. The Cambridgeshire M.P., Captain Briscoe, complained that the pump at Denver was not powerful enough to drain satisfactorily and that it should be updated like that at St. German's installed in 1934. Here at Upware by the 'Five Miles from Anywhere - No Hurry' they are unloading not beer but oil from Ely to keep the auxiliary pumps going. Behind the floods lap the top of Cam banks.

Cambridgeshire Collection

MARCH 1937

The spring tides were the problem again and the river banks of the South Level were being stretched to bursting point in the month of March. The floods hit the headlines and sightseers came from far wide in the new car age. The Hundredfoot bank was under strain, the water as high as the maximum in 1928 and there was a weakness at Cross Water Staunch on the Little Ouse and a tug was sent steaming there carrying 1,000 sacks of clay. The Old West weakened between Earith and Aldreth but the Cam banks held firm. Lorries stood by to evacuate schoolchildren from the villages of Little Ouse and Burnt Fen but the fen people had resolved not to move until they were washed away. Yet only one bank gave way and that was on the Soham Lode at Barway on March 17th. The sluice gates at the entrance to the Ely Ouse had been under great strain and were relieved only by the breach releasing water over a thousand acres. Air force personnel from Mildenhall were sent along with spades but the repairs were put largely in the hands of more experienced men, seen here at the breach with apparatus and clay barges.

Author's Collection

THE BARWAY MENDERS

These men toiled through the bitter cold of that winter of 1937 to repair the Barway breach, one shift during the day, another at night. The Salvation Army in Soham made cocoa for them and had it transported to them in a butter churn carried, as far as possible, in a coal lorry owned by Arthur Bradley of Soham. The Catchment Board engineer in charge was Mr. Taverner. Apart from healing this breach there was a great deal of making good to be done along the bank and the floods were left on the land to avoid further overloading of the river. The dam built here enables the men to work thoroughly and the day was won.

M.R. Barton

Linden End, Haddenham.

No. 4871.

HADDENHAM

And so to the big one, affecting the farmers of this village more than any. Haddenham itself rises to 120 feet above sea level and looking from its peak towards Cambridge gives every impression of a drained sea. Now with a population nearing three thousand, it has many fine houses. It was here that Ovin the Saxon, steward to Queen Etheldreda, founded a church in 673. Linden Close derives from the ancient name for Aldreth where Hereward faced the Conqueror's men, a story still regarded as mythical to many. Haddenham descends gradually by a long road to fen level and on to Earith, this road being Hillrow, leading on to Hillrow Causeway where the worst of the floods occurred in 1947. The story follows.

Cambridgeshire Collection

49

THE ESCAPE ROUTE

Holy Trinity church crowns the isle of Haddenham in 1909. Going up from fen level the winding road seems unending, but you get there into the centre of the village, left to Sutton, ahead to Wilburton and Stretham. Most of the houses and cottages along this route are older than this photograph. The 17th. century Porched House presses close to the road on a corner. The farm taints would have been rich along here at one time. The route offered safety to the Hillrow farmers in 1947 when they had to escape the encroaching floods carrying all they could of stores and chattels, towing implements, looking back with foreboding. The bank had gone, the water could be seen coming.

Cambridgeshire Collection

THE MAN WHO TOOK THE PICTURES

Walter Martin Lane of Ely was born on March 20th 1906 and he died on December 26th 1973 aged 67. He worked for Foster Brothers, Outfitters, of Ely and was a lay preacher whose abiding hobby was photography. He took only his normal time off work to take the photographs of the 1947 floods but was feverishly dedicated to capturing every aspect of them, staying up all night with the army personnel, endearing himself to them as the slightly eccentric amateur in the front line of operations. His endeavours accumulated an invaluable archive stored in the Cambridgeshire Collection at the Lion Yard Library, Cambridge.

Brian Lane

THE THAW

It was a time of post-war austerity. Rationing was still in force and the servicemen were coming home in numbered groups. It was a time of slow recovery and the winter of 1946-47 was severe. January, February and the first week in March were beset by blizzards, rain and strong winds. Then in March 9th the thaw began, hastened by heavy rain. It continued until countrywide some 690,000 acres of land were flooded, 350,000 of them arable. And the fens, needless to say, were to be hit hard. The thaw in the catchment area of the Great Ouse began on March 10th. The discharge of water was soon 50% higher than in previous records above Earith. On the eastern side of the fens the water rose by about eight feet in four days. Cottenham Lode spilled over on March 13th and tugs set forth laden with clay and there was fear everywhere that banks would 'blow in the tow,' meaning in the weakened parts. On Sunday the 16th the southern winds turned to gale force, ultimately to reach nearly a hundred miles an hour. Then they veered south-west, the worst for floods. Then came the first fen breach, the cause of the drown over the fens below Earith, Haddenham, Wilburton and Sutton, seen above.

Cambridgeshire Collections: W. Martin Lane

THE OUSE BANK GIVES

The bank that gave was that of the Ouse coming towards Earith past Over, a solid clay bank twelve feet wide at the top. Farmers were advised to evacuate Over Fen, but they had seen the floods coming. One farmer had to leave a bull behind, supplied with food, but he went to fetch him later in a boat. After dark lights were set up to guide them, hanging on to what they could of goods and chattels. Gangs of men made for the breach, hoping to close it by nine p.m., but they were beaten by the gale hampering their every movement. It was the start of the most serious flooding in the fens. Meanwhile at the fen office in Ely the decision was reached to ask for military help. German prisoners of war were brought in too. Here we see a pile-driver brought into service, on rails laid down by the army. The men draw close for shelter and warmth, lit by floodlight, a momentary breather before throwing themselves back into the task.

Cambridgeshire Collections: W. Martin Lane

ON THE MOVE

Along the Hillrow Causeway men and beasts make for the higher ground of North Hill, Haddenham, the rising waters appearing about them. Charlie Amory perches on the tractor pulling a drill behind it with a bike aboard. Erosion of the peat had left the causeway a little higher above the fields each year, so there was comfort in having that much security for a while. But not for long. The floods from the Over breach reached the flood bank of the Old West River and began to wear at it. The floods rose to six feet higher than the Old West level and on the Monday morning, the 17th, gangs sought to build a high breastwork on the vulnerable Old West southern bank. The troops arrived that night and they worked all through that Monday with the gang, attempting a breastwork on the Northern floodbank. They continued all night into Tuesday morning but the task was hopeless. The farmers could hardly believe the warnings they received for they had never conceived of floods on the scale predicted. A few hours later some were being rescued by boat from upper windows.

Cambridgeshire Collections: W. Martin Lane

ESCAPE TO HIGHER GROUND

Nobody saw or heard the bank give way at Over, but it must have been spectacular. It was happening elsewhere, not far away. Alarm spread near Prickwillow where men worked grimly in the teeth of that gale to secure the banks of the Lark. On Monday 17th the Little Ouse breached, pouring water into Lakenheath and Feltwell fens and another breach in the Ely Ouse occurred near Little Thetford. Two heavy barges were swept through the gap into the floods and the Cambridge-King's Lynn railway was submerged. The flood spread over 2, 000 acres, reaching Stretham Mere. Under stress from the Over breach both banks of the Old West gave way and the rich farmland was soon under a vast, deep lake. This road out from Earith to Haddenham was soon submerged, which gives some indication of the depth, It was a time when horses and tractors shared the haulage on most farms. The exodus was slow here since the loads were as heavy as could be managed with salvaged goods. Implements have been pulled off the fields to higher ground on the right, but it was not high enough.

Cambridgeshire Collections: W Martin Lane

TROOPS ARRIVE

Throughout Tuesday, March 18th the floods continued to deepen. Houses, farm buildings, stacks were submerged and the wind thrashed waves and debris against them until the walls cracked and tumbled. Some straw stacks floated away, some stood firm with rats swarming about them, some scrambling up from within, some climbing aboard. Household chattels and many a poignant souvenir drifted, never to be recovered whole or in pieces. The military geared themselves for a full operation and here the troops have arrived at Earith station, their first priority to help close the gap at Over, armed with all that might be of use to do the job. 'Operation Neptune,' it was called and there were enough men to attend the other imminent crises. The banks of the Hundredfoot were causing alarm and the banks of the Wissey near Hilgay were under stress. These men would need the knowhow of the fenmen working beside them, but they had means at their disposal that would have been unthinkable before the war.

Cambridgeshire Collections: W. Martin Lane

THE BRIEFING

Fenmen in a flood crisis act together intuitively, united in their need and by the urgency of their tasks. The military do things their own way, men acting under orders, even when undertaking something as unmilitary as 'Operation Neptune.' These are mainly a mixture of men seeing out their war service and National Servicemen doing their compulsory two years, but there were plenty of specialists among them being Royal Engineers and Royal Army Service Corps personnel. They had to be given lodgings and Sutton farmer, Bill Read, boarded sixteen of them in his farmhouse, finding them quite happy to sleep anywhere within four walls and a secure roof. It was a happy coincidence that such manpower was at hand for the worst fen flood crisis of them all. Dufflecoats and lifejackets were the order of dress and they were all set for a busy and sometimes hazardous few days.

Cambridgeshire Collections: W. Martin Lane

THE DROWNED FIELDS

With high tides blocking the outfalls, the rivers full to the brim and their banks under great strain it was a matter of preserving those banks and waiting. Banks gave way where weak materials had been used to seal them, or in some cases where penetrations had been made by rats and moles just enough to begin a seepage. Restoring banks was never to be a rush job, but in a crisis such as this caused by the Over breach it was urgent to seal the gap one way or another, then do the job permanently when the conditions allowed. The army proved to have the means, as we shall see. This aerial view looks down on Hermitage Lock with Earith bridge crossing the Hundredfoot on the left. The Sutton road following the bank is under water and the road to the right from the bridge, dry for a short distance, is the causeway to Haddenham which from this point is in Haddenham parish. The waters are silent here but gales were coming back and there was worse to come for the marooned homesteads. Air reconnaissance was another service provided and when W. Martin Lane had need to go to Cambridge to bring back some prints he was offered a lift by air. He was so enthralled by the possibilities of photographing from above that he asked not to be set down until he taken some shots, this being the most successful.

Cambridgeshire Collections: W. Martin Lane.

GEORGE DENNIS'S HOUSE AND FARM

Charlie Bester, who was the parish clerk for Haddenham for more than forty years, had need to contact all those Haddenham farmers stricken by the floods in advance of their receiving possible compensation. Charlie was moved by the modest claim eventually put in by George Dennis, who may have had charity in mind more than need. The claim was returned in disbelief. The country needed these farmers back in business, although the prospects for the year had to be abandoned. George Dennis's house was largely washed away when the gales returned. Meanwhile the floods extended to over 200,000 acres throughout the fens and the Over breach was receiving all the attention hereabouts. It was inspected by engineers of the Great Ouse Catchment Board on Tuesday March 18th when the current was obviously too strong for a barrier attempt. An engineer suggested the army might have the solution to a temporary barrier in the form of amphibian load-carriers, similar to those army Ducks (DUCW's) used in the war but running on tracks. Some of these weighed as much as eighteen tons, unloaded, The army agreed to make the attempt but it was not possible before March 24th eight days after the breach. After many hazards nine of these vehicles loaded with their Sommerfield track, tarpaulins and sandbags formed a rectangular barrier round the breach while gaps were filled with tarpaulins and sandbags and a wall of sandbags placed to complete the job. The men worked through the night and by dawn March 25th the gap was sealed.

Cambridgeshire Collection: W. Martin Lane

ARTHUR THULBON'S HOUSE

On Friday, March 21st the weather worsened throughout the fens. Another south-westerly gale sprang up and houses like Arthur Thulbon's at Hillrow were battered by waves and debris beyond repair. Afloat here and facing the camera are, left to right; Les Few, Bill Allen and Albert Newman who, from his own battered home had rescued one of those old square biscuit tins full of pound notes. A bungalow was built in place of Arthur's house. There was fear of still worse to come. Two-and-a-half miles of the Hundredfoot bank were eroded dangerously by this second gale. There was no longer access other than by water, although the top of the bank was clear of the water. With Sutton the base for the operation, those army 'Ducks' were used to transport straw bales, coconut matting, brushwood and army track and thousands of bags of clay sent from Ely to Sutton by lorry. Day and night the 'Ducks' ferried these materials to the bank until it was sealed. Arthur Thulbon's son Reg still lives near the second bridge at Hillrow.

Cambridgeshire Collections: W. Martin Lane

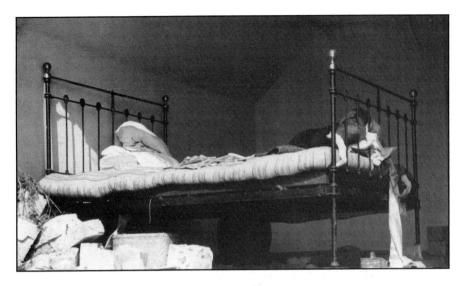

BED BUT NO BREAKFAST

The photographer, minus a telescopic lens, took to the water for this one, entitling it as above. This is Arthur Thulbon's bed, glimpsed on the front cover, and if the bed had been made before the occupants of the house made their escape the rats soon unmade it. Starving, they clawed the bedding to shreds in search of food. In his need to record all he could of this disaster, W. Martin Lane developed an eye for poignant mementoes and telling faces. The floods were still rising here on March 24th, the depth some fifteen feet. The House of Commons seemed at this time more concerned over the loss of food resources than the plight of the fen people or prevention measures against future floods, but that couldn't go on. There were flood problems in other parts of the realm, with the Thames three miles wide in places. Thirty counties had serious flooding by March 17th. Trees blocked the railways, telephone communications were cut off and fifteen people had been killed by the storms. Brigadier E.E. Read, Chief Engineer, Eastern Command, in charge of the Royal Engineers of 'Operation Neptune' received a telegram from a Dutch engineer offering his expertise in the crisis. The engineer, Mr. Kalis, formerly the superintendent of the Wakheiren Gaps, was welcomed. There was much more to be done before the operation was complete.

Cambridgeshire Collections: W. Martin Lane

WALTER NEWMAN'S HAM

It was afloat, a fine ham freed from a chimney breast and there were carrots and beetroot to catch the photographer's eye. He dragged them to dry land and photographed them as a still-life, calling it 'Meat and Two Veg.' Then he strung the ham to this Ely Rural District Waterworks post for another picture and was soon after invited to take the ham away with him for a choice meal. Even at such a time of food shortages and having been assured it would prove most palatable when boiled, W. Martin Lane refused it and the ham was restored to the flood. There were more urgent things on his mind and he just didn't fancy it.

Cambridgeshire Collections: W. Martin Lane.

REG THULBON 'S HOUSE

In the boat are, left to right; Reg Thulbon, George Burton, Arthur Thulbon and Tom Burton pulling away from the crushed house of corrugated iron that had been occupied by Reg. The house was repaired and lived in again but was later demolished. The Thulbon's had bad luck. Arthur's crushed house is nearby on the left. These farmer's spent much time afloat now, hoping to retrieve small belongings and mementoes , ever checking on the damage. They had work to do only if they had livestock safely installed on high ground and standing about looking down on the dismal scene was not in their nature. They had lost their means of livelihood for a year, but they knew this was happening elsewhere in the fens. There had been no drown like this before in living memory and there has never been one since. Things were happening on their behalf. The government agreed to contribute a million pounds to a relief fund and on March 27th the Lord Mayor of London, Sir Bracewell Smith, in a letter to 'The Times' said he had opened a National Distress Fund with the approval of the government to which he had given a thousand pounds and his Mayoress one hundred. Survival was on the cards for fen farmers, at least.

Cambridgeshire Collections: W. Martin Lane.

ARTHUR THULBON AFLOAT

Boats were ever part of the fen farmer's equipment. There were rivers to cross to count cattle on the washes and there was always the risk of floods. Arthur Thulbon looks at ease having surveyed the worst but there was much on his mind. Nobody wanted to concede his home to the elements. J. Cook of Over Fen had insisted: 'I'm not leaving the ship until it goes under,' which it duly did. The Ouse system floods were by far the worst. In the North and Middle Levels the Witham and the Nene caused fewer problems than the Welland. Lincoln was flooded by the Witham but the farmland there and below the Nene had only minor flooding. On March 26th there was a threat to the Witham near Boston where the banks weakened. At 9.16 p.m. the highest of the spring tides produced a 25-feet wall of sea water in the tidal estuary, blocking the outflow of river water. For the next two hours two hundred workers turned out to buttress the danger spots - successfully. The flow of the Welland was badly obstructed at Spalding at that time and the slow release of water into the Wash caused an overflow into the washland. The wide stretch of it near Crowland received an estimated six million tons of water until it became urgent to raise the floodbanks to keep it there. Ice floated on the water on that Sunday of the gale, March 16th, which drove it against the banks causing gaps. For six days gangs of men fought to plug the gaps, then on Friday 21st the eastern bank gave and troops were called to help, The bank gave again farther along, sending a torrent southwards to Thorney, eastwards to Eye and into the fens north and west, but Crowland itself, though encircled, was not affected.

Cambridgeshire Collection: W. Martin Lane

THE FORCE OF THE FLOODS

A picture to dispel any doubts about the depth and force of the water at Hillrow. This is Jack Pake's house on Frank Palmer's farm. Jack was employed by Frank and this tied cottage received, in W. Martin Lane's words, 'a real washing.' Only the shell of the house was left, the front wall being battered away. It was, nevertheless, restored. Never had such an army of workmen and women been brought in to counter flood conditions. Nearly a hundred army vehicles, fully equipped, were used in this area alone and the number of assisting prisoners of war reached a hundred. News of the Southery burst alerted another army of men while elaborate plans were laid to shift the waters once the rivers could accept them. Dutch auxiliary pumps were on their way and National Fire Service pumps were put on standby in London. Fifteen naval salvage pumps capable together of pumping more than 11,000 tons of water an hour and forty smaller pumps were sent to the fens and Yorkshire on March 27th. Fifty-eight firemen with ten heavy units left London for the fens on April 3rd, committed to spending a week pumping out the flood water. The women played their part. Mobile canteens served the workers on the banks and the Women's Voluntary Service revived their wartime re-homing scheme to offer gifts of household needs It was the wartime spirit revived.

Cambridgeshire Collection: W. Martin Lane

BY EARITH STATION

Earith station at the end of Hillrow Causeway was on the Ely-St. Ives line, a casualty of Dr. Beeching in the 1960s. These cottages opposite and 'Midfeather Villas' beyond the shed are still standing. The gale has hit the chimney on the first one and in the second lived the widow, Mrs. Hard, who owned a herd of dairy cows administered by her son, Eric. The water poured like a torrent into her yard. She was elderly and could but salvage all she could from downstairs. In face of the threat Eric had got the herd away to the safe heights of the wartime Mepal aerodrome where they were housed and milked in hangers until the floods had gone. The milking machine was on loan from the Simplex Dairy Company who installed it free of charge six hours after receiving a telephone call from Mrs. Hard. Much wisdom after the event was manifesting itself in the press. Theories about flood prevention in the future abounded and the Middle Level was held up as an example. There was some comfort for the afflicted farmers in the knowledge that the Lord Mayor's Fund, which he had announced over the radio, was mounting rapidly.

Cambridgeshire Collections: W. Martin Lane

BACK ON DRY GROUND

The press displayed many pictures of the fen floods but only one photographer drew close to the victims. To win support for his relief fund the Lord Mayor needed to stir hearts and consciences. A great deal of money was needed to give worthwhile support. Apt studies of the victims were needed to appear in the fund's official appeal book and this one of Mrs. Hard, back on dry ground but looking suitably subdued by her experiences, was used. The cows were ready to return home and all would soon be normal again, with public transport across the road for another dozen years. It was one of W. Martin Lane's moments of captured poignancy. The prettily windowed barn behind still stands although the shed on the right has been replaced. Eric Hard and his wife who lived next door at 'Midfeather Villas,' have since died.

Cambridgeshire Collections: W. Martin Lane

FACES OF THE FUTURE

The floods are receding and these girls just into their 'teens have only the future on their faces. They had known the war, as far as it affected Haddenham; the air traffic from the fenland bases nearby with opportunities, no doubt, to beg gum from the Yanks. The floods have been a novel experience for them, perhaps an uplifting change of scenery, a chance for the photographer to record hope rather than despair on the faces of the inhabitants. The girls are, left to right; Violet 'Bubs' Allen, Phyllis Angier and Betty Morton. Violet (Amory) lives by the Hillrow Causeway today. They would see no crops on the land this season. After the long drying out Bill Read, who farmed below Sutton, recalled one of the strange consequences of the floods when he got back to tilling the land. As he ploughed to the higher ground just above the waters the soil turned over a mass of wireworms such as he had never seen before, they having squirmed their way to safety.

Cambridgeshire Collections: W. Martin Lane

FACES OF EXPERIENCE

In contrast to the bright faces of the young girls are these registering the ordeal of the floods in front of Tom Burton's house well above the flood level in Hillrow. W. Martin Lane took the picture from a 'Duck' giving the faces no time to contrive a smile. Left to right they are: Frank Palmer, Jack Pake, George Fairchild, Albert Newman and Maurice Waddelow with Tom Burton in front and his wife in the doorway. Tom's daughter, Mrs. Joan Hamence lives nearby on the other side of the road below North Hill, a picturesque backcloth, where her late husband was a farmer. Apart from two older men, these are the faces of men unwillingly laid off work, their land out of commission, their property devastated. It was estimated that 200,000 acres of fenland would not be sown that year.

Cambridgeshire Collections: W. Martin Lane

ROYAL VISIT

Concern for the victims of the fen floods was expressed in the far corners of the empire. In Australia the Red Cross had a great response to their appeal for non-perishable items of food and clothing and its National Council had already allocated £50,000 to purchase more and had chartered a ship to send them at once. The state divisions acted independently in support. At home with the floods under control it was time for the King to send an emissary and it was the Duke of Gloucester and his Duchess, travelling by train from Barnwell Manor, their home in Northamptonshire to Bluntisham station on Sunday March 30th. Churned up mud lay about the station which had been the 'entrainment point' for the troops, but the Duke wanted nothing cleaned up for him but the situation in the raw. He travelled to Southery and the Wissey breach and to the Over breach and while having to meet local dignitaries he dismissed formalities as best he could.

Cambridgeshire Collections: W. Martin Lane

ON THE BANK

Having driven by car from their home to the station the Duke and Duchess of Gloucester added a 'Duck' to their means of transport and finally the railed trolley on which they are sitting here on the Ouse bank pointing towards the repaired Over breach. They also got plenty of mud on their boots. There would be floods around for several days yet and it would be months before those flooded out of their homes would be able to return. Massive pumps were being put in place to soak up the flood water when the rivers could take it. Those from Holland were capable of pumping three hundred tons per minute. By April 3rd it was timely for Major-General C.E.N. Lomax, GOC Eastern Command, to send his congratulations to Brigadier E.E, Read, GOC Eastern District, and all his troops on their sterling work in the flood crisis. Ultimately the floods might be seen as a blessing in disguise to the farmers who were enabled through their compensation to rebuild and refurbish their farms considerably. The houses along Hillrow today are relatively new. The local bobby and the vicar had their jobs to do through the crisis. P.C. Pegg would seem to be an apt name for the one and the other just had to be the Reverend Sandberg!

Cambridgeshire Collections: W. Martin Lane

WISSEY BREACH

This was the second dire emergency attended by the military. Local men had been out in force keeping a close watch on the bank of the Wissey near Hilgay. For some thirty hours into the early hours of March 18th they had toiled to reinforce the fifteen-feet high bank above Hilgay Fen, using sandbags and tarpaulins, lighting their way by hurricane lamps. Then half a mile downstream near the entrance to the Ouse at six o'clock on that Tuesday evening the bank burst with a great roar of cascading water which soon spread as far as the Ely-King's Lynn road This is the breach in full spate, the troops helpless to seal the gap against such a current. Their fear was that the flood would rise high enough to cross the road into the Methwold and Feltwell Fens, but a preventative measure had already been taken against this. There were culverts under the road serving the drainage system and these were firmly blocked as a precaution. But now there was another preventative plan afoot.

Cambridgeshire Collections: W. Martin Lane

THE WALL

The Ely-King's Lynn road ran straight for nearly a mile south of Southery and it was seen to be necessary to build a rough wall alongside to prevent the floods from spilling over. Men local and military are seen here filling sandbags for the wall which was to run the whole length of the straight stretch. There was transport aplenty on hand, first bringing the sand then clay from a pit opened for the purpose. The men worked on the wall all through Wednesday 19th March and into the night. Searchlights, RAF field lights and the lamps of auxiliary lighting systems strung between poles were set up along the roadside. Wireless transmitters were used and the women worked tirelessly providing food and drink. The flood waters were rising fast and it was a race against time.

Cambridgeshire Collections: W. Martin Lane

THE BATTLE LOST

Like a scene out of the first world war western front, haste is written all over the construction of this bank against the floods. It is the morning of Thursday March 20th and the men are still busy, for the floods are rising at the rate of six-and-a-half inches an hour. The road was badly cut up by the passage of so many heavy vehicles as the men entered another period of feverish activity raising the wall further using tarpaulins weighed down with earth. Then on the Friday 21st the weather worsened. That second gale sprang up, thrusting the water in great waves against the wall. The sixty-miles-an-hour wind turned it into a loud seafront, but that wall was never breached. Yet the waters won. Under such great pressure one of the culverts gave. It no sooner moved than it burst like thunder, its walls collapsing, the force of the water so great it carried one of the amphibious trucks half a mile across the fen and swept a house out of its path. The people of the fen had been given fair warning and had evacuated to higher ground and the rats were seen everywhere clinging to anything above water.

Cambridgeshire Collections: W. Martin Lane

FILLING THE GAP

With the priority now to seal the Wissey breach the servicemen began as soon as the current allowed by throwing in heavy chunks of stone for a foundation. These servicemen look relaxed as they settle into the job, but the photographer had asked them to turn to him so they are fixing their souvenir smiles. Or perhaps I should say he told them to look at him, for his peremtory tones so impressed the men that they likened him to a sergeant-major. This was hardly the nature of the man. W. Martin Lane was a lay preacher and one hardly given to hellfire sermons. As he stood on this bank by the gap earlier he felt the earth trembling beneath him from the force of the current, a moment that typified his determination to compile a pictorial record of these disastrous floods. This breach and all the others were sealed temporarily, then permanently and all the troops retreated to their headquarters, the job well done.

Cambridgeshire Collections: W. Martin Lane

THE FUTURE

The fens, where life is a continuous battle against flooding, naturally had the worst problems in 1947, but there were problems enough elsewhere. Lives were lost, property damaged and communications were disrupted, the gales causing more damage than the water. Towns caught the floods, if only briefly. In Cambridge the greens and commons and the college Backs were flooded and the view here in St Neots is typical where the water would take its time getting away. Once more the old means of transport works better than the new. From parliament downwards the wise words were coming about what should have been done, but legislating for such as the winter of 1947 was like legislating for earthquakes and volcanoes. Yes, the banks could have been higher and stronger but vaster sums of money than those already set aside for flood prevention were not readily available. There was so much wisdom after the event. Suffice it to say that it was a crisis unprecedented in modern times and there has never been a flood crisis remotely like it since, courtesy, indeed, of an improved system and monitoring but also of the sea. Which is to say that it could happen again.

Cambridgeshire Collection

ACKNOWLEDGEMENTS

Apart from the ever reliable help given by Michael Petty, Chris Jakes and the staff of the Cambridgeshire Collection I particularly wish to thank the following for searching into their memories on my behalf for this book: Bill Read of Sutton, Lorna Delanoy, Joan Hamence and Violet Amory of Haddenham, Charlie Bester formerly of Haddenham but now of Ely, Albert Gee of Thorney, L. Hall of Swavesey and Keith Hinde of Waterbeach. I am also indebted to the Lillian Ream Collection, Wisbech Museum, the Central Divisional Library, King's Lynn, and the Birmingham Library Service.

THE AUTHOR

Anthony Day is a professional landscape painter who also writes. He studied art at the Cambridge School of Art from 1948 to 1952 and at Reading University from 1954 to 1955, thereafter specialising in painting the fen country and its towns, selling his work through dealers in London and East Anglia and mixed exhibitions such as the Royal Academy and the Royal Society of British Artists.

For fourteen years he was art critic to the *'Cambridge Evening News'* but he is now principally interested in writing about country matters and local history. Recent articles by him have been published in *'The Countryman'* and *'Cambridgeshire Life.'* He has assembled a huge archive of photographs of his native village of Wicken which he has used in books, exhibitions and slide-shows and took part in the important *'Fen Archive'* exhibition at the Cambridge Darkroom gallery in 1986, the catalogue of which is now a collectors' item.